Visit us on the Web!
Seussville.com
rhcbooks.com

Educators and librarians, for a variety of teaching tools, visit us at
RHTeachersLibrarians.com

ISBN 978-0-593-64836-0 (trade)

MANUFACTURED IN CHINA
10 9 8 7 6 5 4 3 2 1
First Edition

Dr. Seuss's
WHO LOVES YOU?

Random House 🏠 New York

WHO loves you?
I do! I do!

My heart
GREW THREE SIZES
when I met you.

On days that are wet
and the sun is not sunny,

you **ALWAYS** find ways
to have fun that is funny.

Your smile **UN-SLUMPS** me
when I'm feeling blue.

You are open to change.
I **LOVE THAT** about you!

You are **KIND** to all persons,
no matter how small . . .

...and to be loved by you makes me feel **TEN FEET TALL!**

I find I'm **INSPIRED**
by you every day.
By your actions and thoughts
and the words that you say.

There is no place
I'd rather be

than **HANGING OUT**,
just you and me.

Wherever you may go,
or what the future brings,

I ask that you always remember **TWO THINGS.....**

There is no one alive
who is YOU-ER than YOU.

REMOVE PROTECTIVE FILM

And no one alive

LOVES YOU more than I do!